N 2 C

Enamel Advertising Signs

Christopher Baglee and Andrew Morley

A Shire book

Published in 2005 by Shire Publications Ltd,
Cromwell House, Church Street, Princes Risborough,
Buckinghamshire HP27 9AA, UK.
(Website: www.shirebooks.co.uk)

Copyright © 2001 by Christopher Baglee and
Andrew Morley.
First published 2001; reprinted 2005.
Shire Album 389. ISBN 0 7478 0510 5.

Christopher Baglee and Andrew Morley are hereby
identified as the authors of this work in accordance with
Section 77 of the Copyright, Designs and Patents Act 1988.

British Library Cataloguing in Publication Data:
Baglee, Christopher
Enamel advertising signs. – (A Shire album; no. 389)
1. Enamel signs and signboards – Great Britain – History
I. Title II. Morley, Andrew,
659.1'342'0941
ISBN 0 7478 0510 5

Cover: *A selection of enamel signs. (Top row, left to right) U3X; N2X; U2X; T2X. (Middle row, left to right) N2C; U3X; U3X (above); N1X (below). (Bottom row) N2C; N1GB; N1Bu; XXX. These codes denote the approximate date and size and the manufacturer (where known) of each sign; for interpretation see opposite.*

DEDICATION AND ACKNOWLEDGEMENTS
The authors dedicate this book with gratitude to those enamel sign enthusiasts, mainly
members of the Street Jewellery Society, who have freely provided pictures and
information used in its preparation, and to their families and friends, who have given their
help and encouragement.

Printed in Malta by Gutenberg Press Limited, Gudja Road,
Tarxien PLA 19, Malta.

Contents

Key to age, size and maker of signs illustrated

It is possible to provide only a rough guide, as many of these signs were photographed under conditions that made the taking of accurate measurements impossible. Indicating size can be misleading as the same design was sometimes produced in a variety of sizes, ranging from 18 inches to 8 feet wide (46–244 cm) (such as Sunlight soap £1000 reward), but these look identical in reproduction. Furthermore, accurate dates are impossible because individual designs were often produced over many years, sometimes over several decades. The given dates are therefore a guide only, based on stylistic analysis rather than documented evidence, and indicate when signs may have been designed and the original batch first manufactured. The date of manufacture can be found printed on only a very few signs (for example some Stephens' ink thermometers and Sunlight soap signs). Makers' names are given where known.

U 3 X

Date

L = 1880–1900, N = 1900–1920, U = 1920–1940, T = 1940–1960, X = unknown.

Size (long edge)

1 = 18 inches (46 cm) or less
2 = 18–36 inches (46–91 cm)
3 = 36–60 inches (91–152 cm)

4 = 60–84 inches (152–213 cm)
5 = greater than 84 inches (213 cm)
X = unknown

Manufacturer

B = Bruton, London.
Bo = Boos & Hahn, Ortenberg-Baden.
Bu = Burnham, London.
C = Chromographic Enamel Company, Wolverhampton.
Ca = Campbell, Belfast.
F = Falkirk Iron Company, Falkirk.
Fe = Ferro-Email, France.
Fr = Franco, London.
G = Garnier, London.

GB = Griffiths & Browett, London and Birmingham.
I = Imperial Enamel Company, Birmingham.
IR = Ingram Richardson, Beaver Falls, Pennsylvania, USA.
J = Jordan & Sons, Bilston.
P = Patent Enamel Company, Birmingham.
S = Stainton & Hulme, Birmingham.
W = Willings, London.
X = unknown.

Thus: L 1 C would indicate a sign manufactured late in Victoria's reign, a small sign such as a finger plate made by the Chromographic Enamel Company of Wolverhampton.

The origins of enamel advertising signs

N 3 X

N 2 X

The earliest advertising was a very localised, individual activity, whereby a trader or pedlar would cry his or her wares in the street, or from a shop or market stall. From the seventeenth century a great increase in written advertising occurred. Retailers painted or chalked sales information on boards placed in their shop fronts and windows, which gave more details than the traditional hanging trade signs that for centuries had symbolised for the illiterate the nature of the services and goods purveyed on particular premises. As universal literacy gained ground, more and more newspaper advertisements, printed 'flyers' and pasted-up posters appeared. The development of better roads, of canals and of the railways made practicable the distribution throughout Britain of locally produced goods. For example, biscuits manufactured in Bath or Carlisle, available only locally before 1840, soon became available nationwide. By the end of the nineteenth century branded goods were commonplace, sold pre-packed in printed containers of paper, card and tin, and it became viable to advertise these products locally and nationally with poster campaigns. Poster advertising, originating partly as a vehicle for political propaganda, was brought to artistic fruition from 1860 onwards by luminaries of the medium like Chéret and Mucha, chiefly for promoting theatrical events but also to advertise products as diverse as journals, bicycles and cigarette papers.

The development of the enamel sign, a uniquely permanent form of advertising poster, is a typical case history of the innovative application of developing technologies for commercial use. It occurred towards the end of the nineteenth century, at a point when all the socio-economic influences that made it possible were well established in Britain. In 1857 a Birmingham-based industrialist, Benjamin Baugh, wishing to extend the scope of his trade as a sheet-metal manufacturer, investigated cottage industry enamelling manufactories on a visit to Germany. On his return to England, from 1859 he applied for various patents relating to metal fabrication and enamelling processes based on his observations of established practices in Germany. The Patent Office records show that Baugh managed the Salt's Patent Enamel Works at Bradford Street in Birmingham. This firm had a stand at the 1860 Trade Exhibition in London and secured orders for decorative enamelled sheet-iron panels for interior wall cladding in public buildings. Among its early customers were a railway terminal, the South Kensington Museum (now the Victoria and Albert Museum), several churches and some government buildings in the Far East. During the next two decades Baugh extended the technique of enamelling sheet iron from decorative panels to advertising plates. His customer base for these advertisements so outstripped that for decorative panels that he began to specialise in advertising plates.

The success of this product enabled Baugh to float Salt's as a public company and in 1889 he built a large factory at Selly Oak, Birmingham, customised for the manufacture of enamelled iron signs. This was the world's first purpose-built enamel sign factory and was registered as the Patent Enamel Company. Other entrepreneurs followed suit, first in Britain, then in mainland Europe, the United States and worldwide. In Britain Patent Enamel's main rivals were the Imperial Enamel Company of Birmingham, the Chromographic Enamel Company of Wolverhampton, Jordan & Sons of Bilston, the Falkirk Iron Company, and Burnham's and

N 1 P

Garnier's, both of London, all established during the 1890s. Much of this information is provided by the recollections in the 1960s of Ivor Beard, who had held a managerial post at Patent. Documentary evidence that would have given precise dates, technical and commercial information, and trading records for all these firms were either lost during bombing in the Second World War or destroyed when the companies (with the exception of the two London factories) amalgamated or closed in the 1950s. Documents discovered in the United States, however, indicate that Baugh continued to exert a powerful influence on the formation of new enamelling companies, and that employees of various firms passed on technical information to ex-colleagues who were

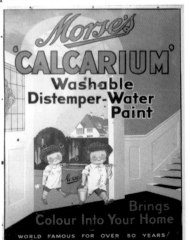

U 3 X

starting up new factories. Details of working methods were jealously guarded and skilled workers were head-hunted by rival companies. An indication of the commercial success of the industry is given by Ivor Beard's recollections of orders of hundreds of thousands of signs and full order books over several decades.

Manufacture, distribution and display

The three main raw materials for sign manufacture – sheet iron, metal oxides and glass – were bought in from foundries and chemical suppliers. The Patent Enamel Company's Selly Oak factory had its own rail sidings, canal arms and on-site stabling for the delivery of the heavy raw materials and despatch of the end product. Ivor Beard's testimony and the evidence of photographs from a surviving Falkirk Iron Company catalogue reveal that the sheet iron was first treated to fit it for use as enamelled signs. An expensive high grade of iron, pure Scotch-wrought puddled iron,

was the metal of choice until, in the 1920s, Armco produced vitreous-enamelling quality steel, a grade of steel sufficiently free of defects for the purpose of enamelling. Initially the metal was 'scaled' in furnaces, stretched, cut, treated in acid baths and sand-blasted to provide a key grip surface. Hand-tooling using hammers, rollers and drills followed. Each dressed, cut casting was dipped, sprayed or 'slushed' with a 'grip' or 'ground' coat of a greyish-white suspension, the consistency of cream, comprising powdered glass (frit), clay and water. The coating was allowed to dry, then the plates were stacked in a workshop fitted with steam pipes, and then fired in a kiln at about 900°C. The hot ware was withdrawn from the kiln and coloured frit was dusted on the surface, forming a continuous layer of enamel. The plates were reheated before the application of each colour in turn. The order of applying and firing colours (each colour achieved by adding a different metallic oxide to the frit) was determined by the temperature tolerance of the oxide. Oxides reaching the required colour at low temperatures were added last. Ideally they were added in the sequence of dark over light, black being the final application.

A page from a catalogue of the Chromographic Enamel Company.

For detailed stencilling or for the application of decals (transferred designs), the plates were allowed to cool so that they could be safely handled, and gum Arabic or cobalt was added to the frit mixture to ensure adhesion to the surface as the plate was taken back to the

A cover of a catalogue of enamelled signs produced by Jordan & Sons.

kiln. The gum base burned out during firing, leaving perfectly detailed, pure enamel images.

There are no surviving archives from any of the enamel sign factories that give information about distribution but labels on the backs of signs, a few contemporary photographs and references in the archives of end-user manufacturers (such as Lever Brothers) give a general indication of the process. Batches of signs were despatched by

Right: *The enamelling department of the Falkirk Iron Company, 1902.*

Left: *Factory workers brushing away unwanted frit through stencils at the Falkirk factory.*

rail, canal and road to distribution depots or to the premises of end-user companies, from where they would be transported to the sites where they were to be erected. Large companies had their own distribution system, such as a fleet of horse-drawn drays, as with Lever Brothers; small companies would hire an independent carrier (such as Pickford's) to transport the signs. Shopkeepers were paid a small annuity to make wall space inside and outside their premises available for the signs. Sometimes a condition of receiving this fee would be that the shopkeeper should clean and maintain the sign. Some companies, like Hovis, employed teams specifically to tour the country maintaining their signs. As the benefits of advertising became more apparent, effort and experimentation were devoted to discovering the optimum use of advertisements. W. H. Lever is reported to have commissioned market research to determine the exact site on a railway station platform that was the most easily and often observed by passengers waiting at, entering and leaving the station.

L 2 I

Left: *A sign erection and maintenance team from Lever Brothers at work, c.1910.*

N 2 X

Design

The earliest extant enamel advertising signs, from the 1880s, comprise simple stencilled words: usually the brand name of a product, the name of the product manufacturer, a simple slogan, and a small cartouche indicating the name of the sign manufacturer. This basic style endured as the staple house style for enamels throughout the remaining seventy or so years of their production. The more colours a sign had, the more it cost to produce. Complex pictorial stencils or chromographically imaged decals cost even more. For example, a surviving catalogue of 1888 issued by the Chromographic Enamel Company offered a four-coloured stencilled-lettering sign with a small multicoloured central picture and offset coloured medallion logo, overall size 60 x 40 inches (152 x 102 cm), for 50 shillings each per fifty. A 30 x 30 inch (76 x 76 cm) square blue-on-white stencilled-lettering-only sign cost 30 shillings each, fifty for 6s 6d each and a hundred for 6 shillings each. The relative colourfulness and

pictorial richness of any enamel are almost always in direct correlation to the sales volume or profit margin of the product advertised. From the start, size was infinitely flexible. The largest plate was determined by the capacity of the kiln in which it was fired, usually no more than 6 or 8 feet (183 or 244 cm) all round. However, assembling several plates, edge to edge, at the destination site could

N 3 X

U 3 X

W. H. Smith's bookstalls have been associated with railway stations since the mid nineteenth century. The company became involved in the control, supply and display of advertising on station forecourts and platforms. Many major companies chose railway sites to promote their products, and enamel signs were a favourite medium for the purpose. Smith's themselves used the one shown above, the newsboy with basket (left) and even had signs warning potential vandals off their advertisements (below)!

N 3 X

Stencils being checked for accuracy at the Falkirk Iron Company.

effectively create larger signs. Workers at Garnier's recall that some such 'assemblages' were so huge that the accuracy of edge-matching could only be checked by laying out prototypes side by side on the road outside the factory. The smallest signs – some just an inch (2.54 cm) across – were destined not for outside use but as permanent labels on pieces of industrial or domestic equipment. Ascot boilers, for instance, displayed a tiny triangular sign in blue and white. Since by far the most popular destination for signs was shop frontages, the size and format were determined by available space. Long horizontal plates measuring 6 feet x 18 inches (183 x 46 cm) were made for the shallow, wide spaces under shop windows, while vertical ones measuring 8 feet x 6 inches (244 x 15 cm) were designed to fit the space between a shop door and the adjacent wall. Most common was a 24 x 36 inch rectangle (61 x 91 cm), capable of having strong visual impact from across a street or at close quarters when fixed to a wall at eye level. Size was not the only variable that the inventive advertisers exploited: profile-shaped (sometimes geometric, sometimes intricately cut in the shape of an object), projecting, hanging, double-sided and pavement 'A' frame variants abounded.

As the medium evolved, sign manufacturers vied for custom by offering ever more complex, detailed and richly ornamented ware. The technique of chromolithography, developed by the printing trade for full-colour images on paper, was successfully adapted for use in enamelling. In this process the sign would usually have stencilled lettering surrounding a chromolithographed pictorial panel, a classic example being the Fry's 'Five Boys' chocolate sign (see title page).

The Falkirk catalogue shows several views of the company's drawing office in which a dozen draughtsmen are employed designing advertisements, then converting the original design to a series of cut stencils. According to the Ingram correspondence (comprising letters to and from Louis Ingram, who set up a factory in the United States), stencil cutters were in short supply in the industry in the 1890s and at that time their trade was among the highest paid. Several signs have survived (for example one made

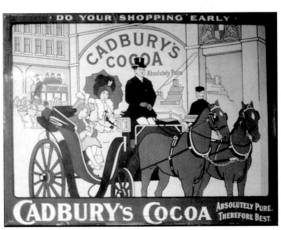

N 3 F

A typical Edwardian corner shop and its staff.

by the Imperial Enamel Company, illustrated on page 7), produced as demonstration pieces of the pictorial effects and colour range offered by sign manufacturers.

As to the quality of design during the period 1890–1914, arguably the heyday of enamel signs, present-day aesthetic standards, which find Victoriana and Edwardiana quaint and attractive, do not equate with the judgement of the time. Advertising art was considered then by anyone with pretensions of taste to be vulgar, brash, crude and merely commercial. Pears' use as a soap advertisement of Millais's *Bubbles*, a portrait of his grandson, caused a scandal in the 1890s and Victorian arbiters of good taste, like Marie Corelli, made public their disdain for such dangerous crossover exercises between high and commercial art. No British graphic artist of the time was awarded a knighthood or other honour that would have signalled public recognition although many fine artists were so honoured from the 1890s onwards. In France the attitude was very different, Chéret receiving the *Légion d'honneur* in 1890. Little surprise then that few British designers' names can be confidently associated with particular enamel signs. Among the exceptions which prove the rule are Sir Alfred Munnings's design for the Bullard's Beer enamel (see page 29), executed when, as a student, he entered a competition set by the Bullard's brewery, and Sir William Nicholson's design for the Rowntree's 'Three Generations' cocoa sign (see page 9), an early work done when he was still an unknown, and even then he and his collaborator James Pryde hid their respectable artistic identities behind the pseudonym of Beggarstaff Brothers. Even as late as the 1970s, Quentin Crisp, reviewing *Street Jewellery* in the September 1978 *Designer*, wrote: 'there is no way in which we can for long keep up the pretence that . . . enamel signs were beautiful . . . enamel signs were hideous'. However, at the time they were produced, these objects, beautiful or hideous, provided a truly democratic, ubiquitous, free-for-all art gallery that cheered the population of industrial Britain. Enamel signs offer an insight into the lives of ordinary people and the commercial practices of a hundred years ago, and they are at the very least delightful objects to collect and ornament modern homes.

Decline

Reasons for the decline of the industry include the interrupted production during the two world wars (when metal and other materials normally used for peace-time purposes were diverted to military use). More damaging, however, was the development after 1950 of other, more effective, less permanent advertising media, most notably street hoardings and television.

There is little recorded evidence against which we can assess the ebb and flow of popularity and use of enamels as an advertising medium. A picture does emerge based on a knowledge of the dates of typestyles and other fashionable design elements, the fluctuation of market prices and the times when goods were newly available, together with an understanding of social history and some demographic research. The authors believe the first enamel signs, produced early in the 1880s, advertised Sunlight soap and Cadbury's chocolate and cocoa; one of the last, produced in the 1960s, advertised Britax safety belts. There would probably have been at least twenty enamel signs for every ten shops in the main shopping street of any British town or large suburb *c*.1935, when many of the earliest

L 2 C

signs would still have been *in situ* and new ones were still appearing in large numbers. Most of these would have advertised confectionery, tobacco products, convenience foods, beverages, cleaning products and pet food. On period photographs of street scenes we have counted as many as twenty signs on one shop's gable end and front. As late as the 1990s, as many as five signs could be seen inside old shops that had withstood changes of shopfitting fashion and kept their ancient interior fittings intact.

N 3 X

N 2 X

N 3 X

U 2 X

N 2 X

At home

Food and drink

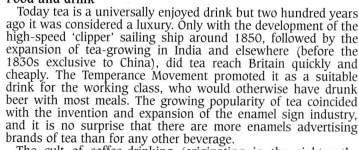

L 1 X

N 2 P

Today tea is a universally enjoyed drink but two hundred years ago it was considered a luxury. Only with the development of the high-speed 'clipper' sailing ship around 1850, followed by the expansion of tea-growing in India and elsewhere (before the 1830s exclusive to China), did tea reach Britain quickly and cheaply. The Temperance Movement promoted it as a suitable drink for the working class, who would otherwise have drunk beer with most meals. The growing popularity of tea coincided with the invention and expansion of the enamel sign industry, and it is no surprise that there are more enamels advertising brands of tea than for any other beverage.

The cult of coffee-drinking (originating in the eighteenth-century coffee-houses) did not spread to the masses until the twentieth century. It was slower than tea to catch on as a domestic drink until the invention in the 1930s of instant coffee and its popularisation in the 1950s. By then the heyday of the enamel sign was over, so few examples advertising coffee exist. Camp (opposite) is a liquid coffee essence, now used mainly as a flavouring agent in baking.

When Justus Liebig first marketed bottled meat extract he became the very paradigm of a nineteenth-century entrepreneur, catering for the new urban proletariat with a cheap food product. The working-class housewife could rarely afford meat, let alone have access to a kitchen in which to roast it to extract juices and dripping. With no home-made beef tea for her hungry family,

N 2 P

N 1 X

N 2 I

N 1 F

L 2 X

N 2 X

U 2 X

U 2 X

N 2 X

N 3 X

or elderly or ailing relatives, she
turned to Liebig's Extract (1865).
It became Oxo in 1899, a brand that has remained firmly inscribed
on British shopping lists ever since, being kept in the public eye
for the first half of the twentieth century by enamel signs and
other printed media (and for the second half by television
commercials). Bovril (1886) has remained a favourite too. There
were originally several other brands (including Ju-Vis, Ex-Ox and
Viandox) until, by successful marketing pressure and a propitious
use of their enamel advertising, Oxo and Bovril secured the

N 2 C

N 1 X

N 1 X

L 3 X

N 1 X

Promotional mugs and spoons for meat-extract products (above) and a detail of the famous Bovril sign (below).

N 1 X

Alas! my poor Brother

N 1 GB

N 2 X

N 1 Bu

territory for themselves. Oxo used several memorable marketing slogans on its enamel and other advertising. The best known is 'The Mighty Atom' (1922, on paper only), but others, in enamel, include 'Splendid with milk for children', 'It's meat and drink to you' and 'Beef in brief'. Bovril also suggested the 'small is beautiful' idea by emphasising the rich concentration of beef in a tiny jar on an enamel sign showing an ox nuzzling a jar of Bovril and lamenting 'Alas, my poor brother!'

As well as hot liquid drinks, from the 1830s, biscuits (based on ships' tack), invented by Fortt's of Bath at the start of the nineteenth century and quickly imitated by others, including Huntley & Palmer's and Carr's, became an 'instant' food with which the corner shopkeeper could stock his shelves.

Frank Smith was reputedly the first manufacturer of potato crisps in printed packets, from 1910 onwards. This innovation was imitated by many others.

The Quaker brand of porridge, founded in the United States in 1877 (Scotts Oats called their version 'porage' in 1914 to distinguish it from that of their competitors), and other brands of breakfast cereal were marketed successfully as health food throughout the world from the 1890s. The Quaker Oats Company ran a campaign in the early 1900s using enamel signs. The sign (opposite) shows the full figure of the 'founder'. Also produced

L 3 J

N 2 X

U 3 X

A promotional bain-marie for cooking porridge.

was a set of enamel signs featuring just the Quaker's hand holding the cereal box, each with a different slogan – 'Of course the clergy eat Quaker Oats', 'Of course athletes eat Quaker Oats' and so on. The signs also stated 'In packets only' as it was then current practice to sell unbranded generic products 'loose' from the boxes, barrels, tubs or vats in which they were delivered to shops. As branded products were sealed in their containers at the factory they could be claimed to be free from the adulteration so feared by the public.

Margarine, first developed in France and Holland in the 1870s, reached the British breakfast table as a cheap substitute for butter a few years later. Butter continued to be sold loose rather than in branded packs well into the 1950s.

Sausages, pork pies, brawn and other offal and meat-scrap-based preparations were cheap but plentiful. Palethorpes and Walls used enamels to advertise their pies and sausages nationally, while smaller firms like Arthur Davy's (below) manufactured, supplied and advertised regionally. The sometimes bland flavour of these foods could be spiced up with one of the many proprietary relishes and sauces. Burma (overleaf) was one of the few sauce manufacturers to issue an enamel to promote its product.

While two other mustard manufacturers, A1 and Keene's, used enamel advertisements, the most widely advertised food relish was Colman's mustard. Folklore has it that Mr Colman made his fortune from what people left on the edge of their plates.

U 3 P

N 2 X

U 2 Bo

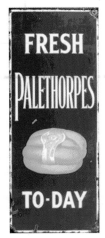

U 2 B

N 2 X

N 1 Ca

N 2 I

L 2 P

N 2 X

T 2 X

Tasks and tackle

During a busy day's shopping, going from one specialist shop to another (all-in-one 'supermarkets' were rare in the nineteenth century), the housewife would have found the chairs with backs formed of enamel signs (opposite) to be a blessing. The shop assistant would take the order, which would then be 'made up' while the customer sat waiting.

When she got home, the daily chores had to be tackled. Serious shopping was rarely done on Mondays, however, as that was the traditional day for doing the laundry. 'Washday' meant Monday throughout Britain until well into the 1950s, after which the gradual introduction of the washing machine made it more practical to do several smaller washes over the course of a week. Traditional washdays consisted of boiling clothes in the 'copper',

agitating them under hot water with a poss stick, then removing and wringing out water using a mangle. Items requiring starch would be separated, starched and re-wrung. The washing would then be taken in a basket (as seen on some of the signs illustrated) to a drying ground – a middle-class semi-detached back

N 2 X

N 1 J

N 1 P

garden, or a working-class 'back-to-back' terrace lane – and pegged on a washing line. 'Good drying weather', sunny with a light breeze, is depicted on Puritan Soap (below). Collecting in the washing was an art in itself, as careful folding made ironing easier. Stretching linen was managed most easily by two people but is accomplished using a chin as a 'third hand' in the Colman's Starch advertisement (below). Additives to the wash water such as blue bags and borax improved the final appearance of the fabrics or protected them, prolonging their usefulness; Reckitt's Bag Blue (opposite), for instance, added brilliance to whites.

Above: A view inside a nineteenth-century shop and chairs with enamel signs incorporated in their backs.

U 3 X

U 1 X

N 1 X

L 1 X

U 2 X

L 1 C

U 3 X

L 1 I

So grim were working conditions for seamstresses in the rag trade that their workplaces were called 'sweatshops'. Back at home there would have been more stitching to be done. For the thrifty family who had saved enough to purchase a Jones or Singer sewing machine, mothers and older sisters could run

N 1 Fe

L 2 P

N 1 X

N 1 X

N 4 X

up any number of night-shirts, slips, jackets and so on, keeping very 'busy' indeed, as the Jones slogan has it (above).

The profit in plain old-fashioned needles and thread was so small that advertising them on enamel signs was not viable. In Britain only a few enamels advertised knitting wool but the most handsome were those made for the German market. An astonishing verisimilitude is achieved in the Eßlinger sign: the old woman, with poor eyesight and fingers crooked with long, hard use, exudes a nobility and inner pride that are quite in contrast with the facile and anodyne appearance of the role models in the Singer, Aquascutum and Jones advertisements (above).

The gritty reality of working life is suggested by the analogy with tough animals (a mangy lion and ruggedly feisty bulldog) on the C. C. & M. boots and shoes signs (above and page 34). By contrast, the Jaeger boots and shoes sign (below) is opulent and luxurious, embellished with sinuous Art Nouveau

X X X

N 2 X

L 2 X

L 3 X

N 2 X

L 3 X

N 2 X

N 1 X

N 2 C

decorative patterning. (Touches of Art Nouveau can also be observed on the Barrett's lemonade sign on page 28.)

From shepherd's cottage to bishop's palace, the Englishman's home was his castle and his wife the chatelaine who looked after it. In most households the man went out to work. Many housewives had paid help but in poor homes the housework would be done by the women and older daughters. With no electrical devices and few mechanical gadgets, everything had to be done by elbow grease. Large quantities of enamels advertised half a dozen brands of metal polish, among them Pelaw, Komo, Brasso, Globe and Matchless, from the middle of Victoria's reign to the start of Elizabeth II's. Women in service and housewives achieved brilliant results, polishing brass and copper objects such as coal scuttles, bedwarmers and candlesticks until they gleamed.

Modern housework relies heavily on spray cleaners and polishes but simple dusting or the application of a generic wax was evidently sufficient before the 1960s, judging by the dearth of early advertising for labour-saving products. Monkey brand soap (page 38) was an all-purpose scouring medium mainly for pans. There are few signs advertising kitchen utensils – the EyeWitness cutlery and Siddons saucepans signs are exceptions. Pots and pans were handed down and buffed up by young housewives.

L 1 X

N 2 C

L 3 X

L 4 X

N 3 X

INSURE WITH THE
LIVERPOOL AND LONDON AND GLOBE
INSURANCE CO. LTD.
ALL CLASSES OF INSURANCE TRANSACTED.
BRANCHES & AGENCIES EVERYWHERE

N 2 X

Established in the Reign of George III.
ATLAS ASSURANCE
COMPANY LIMITED
FIRE AGENCY

N 2 X

REMOVALS AND STORAGE
SAMUEL HILL
DUDLEY & WORDSLEY
HOUSE FURNISHER

L 2 X

ACCIDENTS
OF
ALL KINDS & ILLNESS
EMPLOYERS' LIABILITY ASSURANCE
CAPITAL £1,000,000.
CLAIMS PAID £5,000,000.
INSURED AGAINST
BY THE
RAILWAY PASSENGERS
ASSURANCE CO.
64, CORNHILL, LONDON
AGENT. THE STATIONMASTER

N 2 X

FAMILIES REMOVING
OR
WAREHOUSING
FURNITURE, LUGGAGE, &c
TERMS POST FREE.
TAYLOR'S DEPOSITORY
RANELAGH ROAD.
PIMLICO. LONDON.

N 3 X

Few families at the start of the nineteenth century owned their homes. Most workers rented property from landlords or occupied farm, pit or factory cottages as part payment; if they were lucky, the old retired to charity cottages. As skilled labourers in well-paid jobs aspired to own their own homes but could not afford both their rent and to put aside sufficient savings for their new house, building clubs grew up in the 1770s to assist property purchase. These clubs were the forerunners of the permanent building societies that emerged in the mid 1840s. The Abbey National started in this way, as the National Permanent Mutual Benefit Building Society. Later 'Freehold Land Society' was added to this title. Before universal suffrage the entitlement to vote depended on the ownership of freehold property of a certain value. Home-owning therefore had two benefits: primarily to provide shelter, but additionally to give the freeholder a voice in the nation's politics.

Having made the purchase, the prudent householder would want to make sure that in the event of a catastrophe all was not lost. Thus began dozens of insurance and assurance companies and societies throughout the land. Not only could property and house contents be insured, but also other liabilities

POWELL & POWELL
HOUSE FURNISHERS 18, OLD BOND ST. BATH
AUCTIONEERS AND APPRAISERS
WAREHOUSING AND REMOVALS
FUNERAL UNDERTAKERS AND VALUERS FOR PROBATE
PRACTICAL UPHOLSTERERS AND CABINET MAKERS
ESTATE & HOUSE AGENTS, MONTHLY LIST OF PROPERTIES FREE

L 3 X

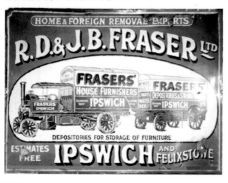

HOME & FOREIGN REMOVAL EXPERTS
R.D. & J.B. FRASER LTD
FRASERS HOUSE FURNISHERS IPSWICH
FRASERS
DEPOSITORIES FOR STORAGE OF FURNITURE
ESTIMATES FREE
IPSWICH AND FELIXSTOWE

N 3 X

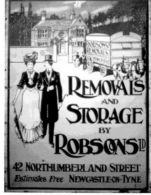

REMOVALS AND STORAGE BY ROBSONS LD
42 NORTHUMBERLAND STREET
Estimates Free NEWCASTLE-ON-TYNE

L 3 X

– life, health, business, livestock and vehicles. Many enamel signs attest to the proliferation of the insurance market (see opposite and above).

Moving house might – for the poor – be a matter of 'moonlighting' with a few possessions on a handcart, but for the wealthier citizen who owned a houseful of belongings it was a more serious matter. Certainly the weightiness of the process was reflected in the imagery on many signs advertising removals firms. Fraser's of Ipswich (opposite) is one of the very best, illustrating a steam engine with one container 'up back', plus another bogey with container on top in tow. The rig's glorious red, white and green livery is echoed in the overall design and lettering of the sign. This colour scheme occurs on other removals firms' advertising, such as the Samuel Hill wagon pictured on the smart-as-paint enamel opposite. Estate agents' 'For sale' signs were also formerly often made of enamelled iron.

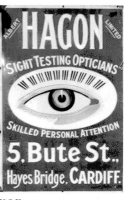

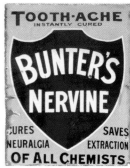

Health and hygiene

Britain's last major plague, the cholera epidemic of 1853, was fresh

in the minds of the people who saw the first enamel advertising signs go up on the streets. Before the National Health Service was introduced, every visit to the doctor or dentist had to be paid for and, for those with no medical insurance policy or cash, charity medical provision was grim. Before advertising regulation arrived to prevent false or misleading claims by manufacturers and marketeers, advertisements for quack cures persuaded hundreds of people to self-medicate. A long-running advertisement for Sunlight soap offered a reward of £1000 to

N 3 GB

N 1 X

U 3 X

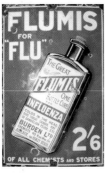

U 2 X

U 2 X

T 2 X

U 2 X

anyone who could demonstrate impurities in the product. The wording was clever because almost by definition soap is pure, being manufactured successfully from raw materials that – while being poisonous, dangerous or just plain smelly in industrial batch form – could be said to be 'free from impurities'. No system of analysis available at the time could have identified 'impurity', even if such a thing as an impurity could have been isolated and unambiguously labelled. So it was with similar, apparently confident and authoritative advertising claims for quack medicines. The message was frequently couched in such a way that even a malady that the potion was supposed to cure was given a name vague enough to avoid successful prosecution for misrepresentation, had anyone the inclination to go to law. One product, Wincarnis, claimed to cure just about everything! As it was, the placebo effect of taking some of these cures was probably

Note the stencilling mistake on the sign below.

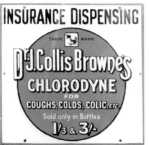

N 1 X

U 2 X

U 2 X

of some benefit to patients whose own metabolisms were bringing about natural recovery. Once biochemists began to gain enough knowledge, techniques and equipment to make accurate analyses, serious concerns about proprietary pills and potions were voiced, and legislation was brought in to control

the abuse of both the advertising language and the physical composition of cures such as Collis Browne's chlorodyne (opposite).

From the 1860s onwards Pasteur's revelations that micro-organisms are responsible for infectious diseases became universally accepted and household cleanliness became a virtue. Disinfectant products such as Izal (opposite) became widely available, as did washable wall paints (for instance, Hall's distemper, opposite, and Morse's distemper, page 5) and effective carpet cleaners (such as Chivers' carpet soap, page 11).

It is notable that sanitary ware seems rarely to have been advertised using the medium of enamel signs (although it was frequently advertised in the printed media). Like kitchen equipment, it is among the few products or services to have this distinction. Maybe no contrivance on the part of advertising agencies could render pots and pans sufficiently glamorous to be profitably advertised, or sanitary ware inoffensive enough to be 'politely' acknowledged at street level.

'Cleanliness is next to godliness' runs the proverb, re-coined in time for the Industrial Revolution by John Wesley in a sermon, and popular throughout the Victorian era. In 1885, just over a century after Wesley's sermon, probably the most famous advertisement of the nineteenth century, and perhaps the best remembered of any era, was designed. It was *Bubbles,* that image of an angelic child, his borrowed clay pipe and bowl of suds in hand, watching the bubbles that he has

L 3 X

N 4 P   N 4 P

SWAN WHITE FLOATING SOAP
ABSOLUTELY PURE

L 4 X

blown float heavenward. Contrary to popular opinion, the painting was not commissioned by the soap manufacturers Pears but was purchased by them from the painting's first owners, the *Illustrated London News*, who bought it in order to produce a promotional 'give-away' poster campaign. The original painting, a portrait of his grandson (1885), was by Sir John Everett Millais, a lion of the British fine art establishment, sometime President of the Royal Academy and a founder member of the Pre-Raphaelite Brotherhood. There is a division of opinion as to whether or not Millais approved of his work being adapted for use as an advertisement.

Whatever his feelings, contemporary debate about the issue has left us with several interesting observations regarding the relative merits of fine and commercial art. Prince Albert's Great Exhibition of 1851 had, as one of its precepts, the improvement of the quality of design in manufacturing, and the Victoria and Albert Museum was intended as a repository of excellence in the applied arts to encourage high standards among commercial artists. Despite these early attempts to heighten the prestige of and remove the stigma from commercial art, 'advertising' has remained a dirty word when associated with 'art'.

Gardening, pets and leisure

Growing your own produce was a sensible and logical activity for hard-up families newly moved from the countryside to the city. If there was no cultivatable garden

N 1 C

N 1 C

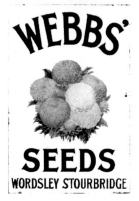

N 2 C   N 2 P   U 2 X

attached to the home, plots could be rented from the burgeoning allotment growers' associations, which were well established throughout Britain by 1900. Seed merchants had large specialist shops in every town and city, catering for the needs of smaller communities. Their wares were displayed in season in colourfully printed packets on specially constructed point-of-sale devices in hardware stores. The tall, narrow enamel signs illustrated opposite (like the five similarly proportioned signs for Stephens' inks illustrated on page 36) would have flanked the shop doorway or else have been situated on either side of the main shop windows.

U 2 X

Agricultural tools, manure, guano fertiliser, cattle feed, patent medicines for animals, lawnmower sharpening services and other gardening paraphernalia were advertised using enamels.

Eventually most defunct enamel signs became scrap metal and were thrown away. However, some were recycled by thrifty gardeners as shanty walls, supports for compost heaps, leek trench dividers, anti-rabbit fencing and potting-shed roofs. This secondary 'life' of street jewellery in allotment gardens was a happy chance that enabled hundreds of specimens to survive destruction.

Household pets have been popular in Britain since animals were first domesticated in the Stone Age. Originally dogs and cats were kept to control vermin, but eventually specific breeds were developed for hunting or herding, or as companions for the young and the elderly. These true pet varieties might be kept in the home alongside caged songbirds such as linnets and larks, long before budgerigars arrived from the antipodes in the eighteenth century. The movement of the greater part of the population to the cities meant that previously commonplace food from the wild and offal by-products from home butchery were no longer available. Butcher's offal was in demand to feed poor humans; thus the trade in specialist pet foods began. As seems to be the case with most other products for which enamel advertising signs were made, a rash of minor manufacturers, represented now by a few scarce examples (such as Lowe's Carta Carna), were pushed

L 2 X

A pet shop with in situ signs photographed in the 1990s.

U 2 X

U 3 X

T 1 X

N 3 X

T 3 X

T 1 X

T 1 X

T 2 X

T 2 X

N 2 X

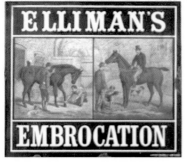

L 2 C

out of the market by the most successful firms. In the case of pet food, Spiller's and Spratt's were the largest producers and the most prolific users of enamels. Spratt's advertising campaign, using the letters of the product name modified to represent variously a Scottie dog, a cat, a budgerigar and a goldfish, must count among the cleverest, most economical uses ever devised of typography as a selling tool. Spratt's, Spiller's and Thorley's also widely advertised their products for farm animals using enamel signs. Thorley's Ovum Poultry Spice, Spratt's Patent Chicken Meal and Elliman's Embrocation are examples of advertising that cross the border between the commercial and domestic markets.

It may be of some significance that when street jewellery had all but disappeared from the streets of Britain, the surviving examples were nearly all *in situ* on pet shops.

Music, sport and exercise
Before radio and television, home entertainment for the masses meant parlour games and music. Strangely, there appear to be no enamels advertising the

N 2 X

U 1 X

U 2 X

N 3 P

U 1 X

N 2 X

U 2 X

T 1 X

hundreds of boxed board games such as 'Halma', 'Sorry' and 'Ludo', or the kit games like 'Lotto' and 'Monopoly'. Perhaps the manufacturers of these were aware, or afraid, of the ephemeral nature of fashion and chose the more disposable, inexpensive forms of advertising, like paper posters and show-cards.

However, more expensive items like gramophones and 78 rpm records were widely advertised using enamel signs, especially by HMV. Other recording companies issued enamels too, and the *trompe-l'oeil* shiny groove of the record reproduced in enamel seems to have had special appeal. Radios were costly status symbols in their early days, and many manufacturers vied for the several guineas needed to purchase one.

There was a time when every respectable home had a piano (usually an upright) or a harmonium, around which the family could gather in the evening to sing popular songs, and hymns on Sundays. Signs issued by local music shops (like Pohlmann's) advertised that they sold keyboard instruments; there are also rare examples of enamels issued by piano manufacturers such as Steinway. Brass bands were widespread, but only a few enamels advertising Boosey & Hawkes brass instruments have survived.

The popularity with the British public for angling, tennis and cycling, all cross-gender sports and hobbies, has never waned. Cycling produced some of the most elaborate and stylish poster art during *la belle époque* in France and inspired a huge crop of enamels in Britain, almost rivalling in numbers and variants those advertising newspapers and tobacco products. The Rudge Whitworth sign was made with a blank white rectangle into which the name of the local supplier was stencilled individually (in this case G. Groombridge; see also the same method evident on the Marmet pram sign on page 31).

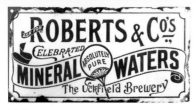

L 2 X

N 2 IR

T 2 X

L 2 X

Away from home

The sweet shop

N 1 X

In Britain's booming industrial towns and cities, more and more specialist outlets joined the 'general dealer' type of corner shop to serve the busy, thriving communities surrounding the factories. Butchers, cobblers, haberdashers and tobacconists all had signs, which could be located on the shop's gable end, above and below the fascia, on the entrance portico wall, projecting into the street, suspended from metal brackets, on 'A' frames set outside daily, and on walls and counters within. Quite often more than one of the same sign would be placed side by side or one above the other. This had the double benefit of hammering home the message and of keeping the competition at bay!

Sweet shops have now mostly disappeared although they were as numerous as other specialist shops. Some still survive as newsagents-cum-tobacconists, where the obligatory ice-cream freezer is still a feature, and – although dandelion and burdock has now largely disappeared –

traditional Tizer and Coca-Cola (respectively over fifty and a hundred years old) are still available. Fry's 'Five Boys' chocolate (see title page) was a particular favourite among the many brands of confectionery that have now disappeared, but other long-established brands are still produced.

Far left: *Annie Godward's sweet shop in Nottingham, photographed in the 1970s.*
Left: *Ancient and modern signs above and below a shop window in Bath.*

N 1 X

U 3 X

U 2 X

L 2 X

U 2 X

U 3 X

U 2 X

Rowntree's fruit pastilles, for example, have Queen Victoria's royal warrant as proof of their extraordinary longevity.

Alcohol and tobacco

Unless the housing estate had been built by a teetotal magnate for his workers or was erected on church lands, most industrial terraces had at least one public house to every half dozen or so 'rows', plus several alehouses outside every factory gate. Add to these several local inns, a handful of working men's clubs or 'friendly society' premises, and a few off-licences, and the extent of the alcohol-rich social life of working-class industrial Britain is clearly evident.

Inns and pubs abounded in rural areas too and had a history that long predates the Industrial Revolution. Local breweries once proliferated but were eclipsed for a few years after the Second World War until the Campaign for Real Ale and natural enthusiasm put them back in business.

U 2 X

U 2 X

N 2 X

U 2 X

U 2 X

U 3 X

U 2 X

U 3 X

Nearly all the big national breweries and distilleries issued large quantities of advertising material, including enamel signs. The form of on-premises advertising at which the breweries excelled was the pub mirror, many of which still survive in pubs and hotels. The survival of enamels *in situ* is less common, but attempts were made in the 1970s and 1980s to reverse the bland standardisation of pubs that had taken place from 1950 to 1970 by recreating old-fashioned bars. These 'theme' pubs were modelled on genuine surviving examples where landlords had collected items to do with the name of the pub, or the area, local industry, popular sport and so on, and which had become minor museums of ephemeral trifles. Attempting to reverse the fashion for flock wallpaper and swirly carpets that spoilt so many pubs after the Second World War, design companies were brought in to recreate an 'authentic' ambience and would as often as not festoon the newly dark-stained plywood snugs and saloon bars with old bottles, mangles, stuffed wart-hog heads and the like. Enamel signs often found a place in these decorative schemes. Unfortunately they were rarely installed with any regard to authenticity. They were either treated with

L 1 X

N 2 X

N 1 GB

N 2 X

undue reverence, as if they were oil paintings, hung up in frames and carefully spaced, or else they were crammed edge to edge, with no thought to the relevance of the products advertised. In original public houses normally no more than three enamel signs would have been displayed in any one pub, advertising beer, spirits and smoking products.

X X X

Above: *Enamel signs at the Crich Tramway Museum.*

Travel and holidays

The few remaining factories that once manufactured enamel advertising signs now use the same skills and plant to make scaled-down reproductions of signs (or, rather, mutant versions of them) for the nostalgia trade. A rough guide to identifying 'repro' enamel signs is that the back is a uniform black, and there is either no maker's name, or a clearly modern maker's name incorporated in the design. Reproductions are usually quite small and have a rather 'greasy' feel to the enamel. Enamelled steel is still used to make information signs such as passenger information maps for local authorities and transport companies. Some of the same customers also commission wall-cladding panels of brightly coloured enamelled steel to line station platforms. On the London Underground, enamel circle and bar station-name totems like the Westminster example can still be observed. Look

U 2 X

U 1 X

U 2 X

N 3 X

out for several variations of this format, including a solid red disc version, depending on the age of the sign. Many traffic information signs and tram- and bus-stop signs, like those from Crich Tramway Museum, Derbyshire (page 31, centre right), were once made of enamelled iron.

U 2 X

Journeys were often long and arduous, so that items of confectionery would have been welcome treats *en route*. The red triangle in the Rowntree's Motoring Chocolate advertisement (page 31) even imitates a traffic information sign.

The most famous of all British advertisements for holidays is John Hassall's 'Skegness is so Bracing', issued by the London & North-Eastern Railway in 1908. It was just one of hundreds of paper posters advertising places to visit that appeared on national railway and London Underground platforms from the late nineteenth century onwards. Although occasionally a successful paper poster was reworked as an enamel (as in the case of the Beggarstaff Brothers' 'Three Generations' Rowntree's cocoa advertisement of 1896, page 13), no enamel version of Hassall's 'Skegness' is known. At least two of his other designs survive in the enamel medium, advertising Morse's distemper (although not the Morse's distemper

U 1 X

N 3 X

X X X

U 2 X

N 4 X

U 5 X

sign reproduced on page 5, the designer of which is unknown).

Illustrated here are four signs which, unlike most of the illustrations in this book, are not in the strictest sense advertisements. Two of them are directional signs (Llandudno and Great Yarmouth Pleasure Beach), one is an instruction plate from the sort of fortune-telling machine commonly found in seaside amusement arcades (opposite page), and one (New Palace Pier at St Leonard's) seems to be an on-site nameplate. The *Daily Sketch* sign 'There First' shows a seaside scene and is thus in the holiday spirit, as is the Irish Sweepstake sign, redolent of a day at the races.

The signs advertising the Queen's Hotel, the Cornish Riviera and Grand Pleasure Tours are all lavishly detailed with incident and information. More than a hundred place-names are included on the Cornish map; a dozen holidaymakers and a convertible limousine are pictured on the promenade before the Queen's Hotel. A coach and four, a twin-funnelled cruiser and an engine of the London & North-Western Railway with three Pullmans in tow seem to travel at speed across the Grand Pleasure Tours sign.

Work and workwear

It used to be second nature to a manual worker to doff his cap to any stranger who, judging by his apparel, appeared to be his

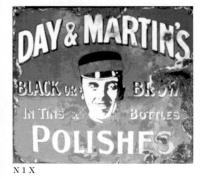

U 3 X

U 2 X

U 3 X

social superior. The class system was ingrained in British society at every level, and clothing was the chief visual reminder of that demarcation between the rich and poor, the upper, middle and working classes, between military and civilian, servants and gentry, and young and old. The gentleman to whom the worker doffed his cap would likely be wearing a top hat, bowler or sporting headgear such as a straw hat or deerstalker; everyone wore a hat, as evidenced in many of the illustrations in this book. The Day & Martin's shoe-shine boy, perhaps an employee of an hotel, wears a peaked kepi in the style of a servant's uniform (page 33). The schoolboy who earns his pocket money by cleaning the boots with Cherry Blossom (opposite) wears a school cap; his clog boots and tweed knickerbocker suit single him out as a state-school pupil (the Eton collar was common to all schoolboys at this period). Two boys wearing public school uniforms or 'Sunday best' are seen larking about with unashamed glee on the

N 1 X

Metal plates being processed by workers wearing flat hats and hob-nail boots (Falkirk catalogue, 1902).

N 4 X

U 2 X

Wellington Journal & Shrewsbury News.
Read by a quarter of a Million.

500 Situations Vacant and Wanted.
Advertised every Saturday.

"I did and I'm Suited!" says Mary

L 2 X

N 3 C

L 4 X

surrealistically huge Eton collar (Robin, page 33). The maid (Wood-Milne, above) evidently has to scrimp and save by doing a little home cobbling, using patent boot menders, to lower the cost of maintaining her uniform.

Many examples of women at work can be seen throughout this book. There are washerwomen and laundry maids (page 17), nurses (Wincarnis and Jeyes' fluid, pages 21 and 22) and housemaids, one on the arm of a policeman (*Wellington Journal*, above). Child labourers include the cheery Walter Willson's shop assistant (opposite), dressed in appropriately hygienic white overalls and mob-style cap. There are little Art Deco decorative motifs on this sign, which help date it to the years between the two world wars, just as Art Nouveau patterns on the Jaeger boots sign (page 18) indicate that it was produced between 1880 and 1914.

Greater literacy came as part of the enormous cultural leap that served and was served by the Industrial Revolution. It enabled mass employment for clerks and secretaries, plus supervisory, administrative, legal and managerial careers for thousands of others. To become a white-collar worker was a route out of the working class and was regarded as a step up the social ladder.

N 2 J

STICKS QUICKLY

N 2 P

U 2 X

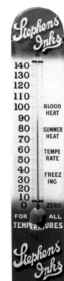

N 4 J

N 3 J (all five)

U 1 X

It was deemed less taxing than manual labour. But besides the practical advantages of literacy, millions also discovered the pleasures to be had from the skill. The improved status afforded to the literate is shown in the signs opposite, featuring a courtroom scene and a government office (*John Bull* and *Passing Show*). People read periodicals (opposite and page 25, *The Field*) and novels by writers such as Sir Walter Scott (pictured in sepia, opposite), whose famous Waverley novels gave their name to pen nibs by MacNiven & Cameron (above and opposite). The names of the Pickwick and Owl nibs evoke the literature of Charles Dickens and Edward Lear. They feature in a rhyme probably coined by a junior

Draughtsmen at work in the drawing office of the Falkirk Iron Company.

U 2 X

N 2 X

N 1 C

L 2 C

worker in an Edinburgh advertising office not dissimilar from the Falkirk drawing office illustrated. It ran:

> They came as a boon and a blessing to men,
> The Pickwick, the Owl and the Waverley pen.

Many stationery requisites were advertised on enamel signs. Perhaps the most celebrated was Stephens' inks, whose enamel advertising thermometers were very widespread. They were manufactured in several sizes and had instructions glued to the back. The thermometer illustrated on the opposite page is unusual in that it has an inky blue coloration top and bottom.

N 2 C

Collecting enamel signs

N 2 X

There is, as with any collectable item, a floating market in which enamel signs change hands between dealers and collectors in antique shops, flea markets, auto jumbles and especially private specialist dealer sales. However, the patient scouring of likely and unlikely locations creates most big collections. Signs do appear in bric-à-brac and antique shops, but usually at true market values. Car-boot sales and bottle or 'advertique' collectors' fairs are normally the best places to find signs at good prices and in various conditions to suit one's pocket. Sometimes local, postal and internet auctions have enamels in their catalogues, but the involvement of serious collectors or dealers may inflate prices. The authors recommend that enamels found *in situ* should be left where they are, so that they can remain as environmental treasures for everybody to enjoy.

The collectability of signs and their consequent monetary value vary according to circumstances. With a mass-produced object such as a sign, rarity is hard to establish, as occasionally a large hoard of a particular sign is discovered in a warehouse where it has lain, well preserved, for years. Even when a sign turns up having been re-used for building material in a garden shed or compost heap, or buried in a rubbish dump, it may be in good condition: the enamelled iron sign can survive remarkably well.

For most serious collectors one factor overrides all others – the condition of the sign. A mint sign, or one with only minimal damage (such as flaking of the enamel around the screw holes, or slight chipping or corrosion around the edges), is highly prized. But if it is visually unexciting, even a mint condition sign is undesirable. A perfectly preserved old specimen of a two-colour sign with simple lettering and no illustration, and advertising a dull and mundane product, will not enhance a collection. Illustrated signs of a conveniently small size, say 36 inches (91 cm) square or smaller, with lots of bright colour and complex, ornate or stylised lettering, have far more appeal and a higher value.

Although most shop fascias have been renovated and modernised, leaving no room for, or trace of, enamels, a few museums of bygones have on display reconstructions of street scenes of earlier times which include many examples of enamelled signs. There are also abundant photographic records of signs *in situ*, stored in local history archives and elsewhere, to which the enthusiast can refer.

The best way to get to know other collectors is to join the Street Jewellery Society, which has a membership of over a hundred dedicated collectors who buy, swap and sell enamel advertising signs. Beware of addiction: once you own an enamel sign you are likely to want others. If you decide to form a

Signs still in situ on the right side of a double-fronted pet shop (photographed in the 1990s). The upstands are entirely clad with Spratt's enamel signs.

collection, why not base it on one of the themes in this book? Good hunting!

The Street Jewellery Society: 6 Crossley Terrace, Fenham, Newcastle upon Tyne NE4 5NY; website: www.streetjewellery.com, www.streetjewellery.org, www.streetjewellery.co.uk

Restoration

Each sign should be checked over for rust damage on the front and back. If it has survived with the enamel intact, a very rare occurrence, then no action need be taken apart from cleaning with an appropriate cleanser (scouring paste and warm water applied with a cloth for mild surface dirt; wire wool and scouring powder, with frequent water sluicing, to shift deeply ingrained dirt). Great care must be taken with delicate transfer and lithographed areas, and with certain black lettering and outline overlays. Rusted areas should be cleaned with a rust-removing chemical agent, steel wool or emery and immediately sealed or treated with oil, anti-rust paint or underseal. Broken and chipped enamel cannot be satisfactorily replaced except in small areas on a good metal surface, but even so the process requires complex equipment and technical skill. A reasonable substitute for lost metal and enamel is car body filler and fibreglass.

L 1 X

N 1 X

N 2 X

N 2 C

N 3 J

Further reading

Baglee, Christopher, and Morley, Andrew. *Street Jewellery.* New Cavendish Books, 1978; revised and enlarged edition, 1988.
Baglee, Christopher, and Morley, Andrew. *More Street Jewellery.* New Cavendish Books, 1982.
Brunner, Michael. *Encyclopedia of Porcelain Enamel Advertising Signs.* Schiffer, USA, 1994.
Conradson, B., and Nessle, O. *Svenska Skylatar.* LTS, Stockholm, 1980.
Courault, P., and Bertin, F. *Email and Pub.* Editions Ouest-France, 1998.
Curtis, Tony. *Advertising Antiques.* Lyle Publications, 1993.
Hansen, John Juhler. *Gadens Blikfang.* Forlaget Jelling, Denmark, 2002.
Riepenhausen, Alex. *Blechplakate.* F. Copenrath, Germany, 1979.
Stakenborg, J., and van Zadelhof, J. *Emaille Borden.* Uiteverij de Viergang, Holland, 1979.
Wlassikoff, Michel. *Les Plaques Emaillées Publicitaires.* Galerie PEP, Paris, 1983.

Places to visit

Beamish, North of England Open Air Museum, Beamish, County Durham DH9 0RG. Telephone: 0191 370 4000. Website: www.beamish.org.uk
Black Country Living Museum, Tipton Road, Dudley, West Midlands DY1 4SQ. Telephone: 0121 557 9643. Website: www.bclm.co.uk
Blists Hill Victorian Town, Madeley, Telford, Shropshire TF7 5DU. Telephone: 01952 583003. Website: www.ironbridge.org.uk
Bluebell Railway, Sheffield Park Station, near Uckfield, East Sussex TN22 3QL. Telephone: 01825 720800. Website: www.bluebell-railway.co.uk
Brewhouse Yard Museum, Castle Boulevard, Nottingham NG7 1FB. Telephone: 0115 915 3600.
Cadbury World, Cadbury Ltd, Bournville Lane, Bournville, Birmingham B30 2LU. Telephone: 0121 451 4159. Website: www.cadburyworld.co.uk
Flambards Village Theme Park, Helston, Cornwall TR13 0QA. Telephone: 01326 573404. Website: www.flambards.co.uk
How We Lived Then, Museum of Shops and Social History, 20 Cornfield Terrace, Eastbourne, East Sussex BN21 4NS. Telephone: 01323 737143.
The Linden Tree Public House, Linden Hall Hotel, Longhorsley, Morpeth, Northumberland NE65 8XF. Telephone: 01670 500000. Website: www.lindenhall-hotel.co.uk
London's Transport Museum, Covent Garden, London WC2E 7BB. Telephone: 020 7379 6344. Website: www.ltmuseum.co.uk
Milestones – Hampshire's Living History Museum, West Ham Leisure Park, Churchill Way West, Basingstoke, Hampshire RG21 6YR. Telephone: 01256 477766. Website: www.hants.gov.uk/museums
Montacute TV, Radio and Toy Museum, 1 South Street, Montacute, Somerset TA15 6XD. Telephone: 01935 823024.
National Cycle Collection, The Automobile Palace, Temple Street, Llandrindod Wells, Powys LD1 5DL. Telephone: 01597 825531. Website: www.cyclemuseum.org.uk
National Motor Museum, John Montagu Building, Beaulieu, Brockenhurst, Hampshire SO42 7ZN. Telephone: 01590 612345. Website: www.beaulieu.co.uk
National Museum of Gardening, Trevarno Estate Gardens, Crown Town, near Helston, Cornwall TR13 0RU. Telephone: 01326 574274. Website: www.trevarno.co.uk
National Railway Museum, Leeman Road, York YO26 4XJ. Telephone: 01904 621261. Website: www.nrm.org.uk
National Waterways Museum, Llanthony Warehouse, Gloucester Docks, Gloucester GL1 2EH. Telephone: 01452 318200. Website: www.nwm.org.uk
Severn Valley Railway, The Railway Station, Bewdley, Worcestershire DY12 1BG. Telephone: 01299 403816. Website: www.svr.co.uk
Shambles Museum, Church Street, Newent, Gloucestershire GL18 1PP. Telephone: 01531 822144.
The Stephens Collection (Stephens Ink Museum), Avenue House, East End Road, Finchley, London N3 3QE. Telephone: 020 8346 7812. Website: www.london-northwest.com/sites/stephens
Ulster Folk and Transport Museum, 153 Bangor Road, Cultra, Holywood, County Down, Northern Ireland BT18 0EU. Telephone: 028 90 428428. Website: www.nidex.com/uftm
York Castle Museum, Eye of York, York YO1 9RY. Telephone: 01904 687687. Website: www.yorkcastlemuseum.org

The authors would be interested to learn of any other places with good displays of enamel advertising signs.